MW00364383

the little book of
KINDNESS

Hardie Grant

QUADRILLE

Kindness

noun

1. The quality of being friendly, generous and considerate

Modern Online Dictionary

Kindness

noun

1. Good offices, friendly actions, beneficence, charity etc.*

* Note the slight difference between the two definitions. The older definition associates kindness with activity rather than as a general characteristic.

New English Dictionary, 1781

What is kindness?

1. The sympathetic knack of observing the emotions of others and responding thoughtfully

2. The instinctive ability to tend to the needs of others

3. The awareness of humanity's desire to make meaningful connections with one another

4. The blending of our needs and desires with others in a mutually beneficial manner

5. The act of buying a mate a coffee

Kindness: synonyms

Altruism

Benevolence

Compassion

Open-heartedness

Philanthropy (love of mankind)

Solicitousness

Sympathy

Understanding

True kindness involves the kind giver to approach the whole world with kindness. Kind people practise kindness to themselves, to others, to animals, to the planet.

"Kindness is more important than wisdom, and the recognition of this is the beginning of wisdom."

THEODORE ISAAC RUBIN

It is now increasingly understood that no matter how fabulous our career, body, Instagram account, social life, if we don't practise kindness, happiness will elude us.

Being kind = being happy

Being good to others = feeling good yourself

Being kind to yourself = being able to be kind to others

"Kindness is a language which the deaf can hear and the blind can see."

MARK TWAIN

Kindfulness

As if mindfulness wasn't zen enough, wellbeing experts are now suggesting that mindfulness is just a tad too introspective. It's only by looking out into the world to see where we can be of use, that true tranquillity will be attained. Kindfulness aims to achieve equilibrium between self-care and kindness. By connecting with, and going easy on, our own frailties and faults, it allows us to nurture and consider others as we would wish ourselves to be treated.

How to harness the power of kindfulness

1. When you make a mistake, don't buy a ticket to the guilt trip. Let it go

2. When others make a mistake, let that go too

3. Treat yourself on a daily basis

4. Treat your friends well on a daily basis: a complimentary note, a genuine smile, time to listen

5. Acknowledge when you've taken a wrong turn. Be honest and try to set yourself right

6. Say sorry to others. If you've snapped or had a sulk, fess up and apologise

7. Give yourself time. Set the alarm 10 minutes earlier so you're not chasing your tail

8. Give others time. Leave the house 10 minutes earlier so you're able to stop and chat to the those you meet

9. Help yourself. If you are repeatedly getting in a mess over an issue, ask others for help

10. Help others. If you see your friends or family getting into difficulties, step forward and ask if there's anything you can do to help

Days to celebrate kindness

21 Jan – National Hug Day

7 Feb – Send a Card to a Friend Day

16 Feb – Do a Grouch a Favour Day

17 Feb – Random Acts of Kindness Day

22 April – Earth Day

28 April – Global Pay It Forward Day

30 July – World Friendship Day

21 Sept – International Day of Peace

13 Nov – World Kindness Day

20 Dec – International Human Solidarity Day

*"There's no use doing a kindness
if you do it a day too late."*

CHARLES KINGSLEY

Decide to be kind to everyone you meet just for one day. See what happens. If it goes well, do it again tomorrow.

Five random acts of kindness

1. Invite someone to go in front of you in a queue

2. Offer to babysit for free

3. Fill in those annoying customer service surveys; they really can benefit the person who helped you

4. Learn the name of the barista who makes your coffee every morning

5. When friends are gossiping about someone, be the person who offers a kind word in their favour

We are kind because we are all human

Once the humanity of all people around you – not just the ones you like – is recognised, treating people without kindness seems monstrous. Understanding that our fellow travellers are as frail, sensitive and fallible as we are, helps us to approach interactions with thoughtfulness and kindness. After all, that is how we, as fellow humans, would wish to be treated.

"A part of kindness consists in loving people more than they deserve."

JOSEPH JOUBERT

We have a nature towards one another

Recognising the common humanity of those around us lies at the heart of being kind. The 19th-century essay writer William Hazlitt put it beautifully when he described walking along the Somerset coast with the poet Coleridge. They met a fisherman who told them about a dreadful storm the day before and a boy who had been washed out to sea. He and other fishermen, at great risk to their own lives, took to the storm-tossed seas and attempted to save the boy.

The fisherman explained their motivation simply, 'We have a nature towards one another.'

FRANK CARR
Essays of William Hazlitt

" Every man must decide whether he will walk in the light of creative altruism or in the darkness of destructive selfishness."

MARTIN LUTHER KING, JR.

The human heart is a wonderful
tool – it tells us instantly when
we've been unkind.

That blush, the thud in the chest,
the lurch of shame in the stomach.
The fact that our bodies respond so
physically after we've committed
a (no doubt accidental) act of
unkindness demonstrates how the
human natural condition prefers
kindness to cruelty.

"If you can't feed a hundred people, then just feed one."

MOTHER TERESA

Snowdrifts' worth of studies have connected increased acts of kindness with enhanced happiness. If you can't be kind to others for their sake, be kind to others for your sake.

After studying a number of Japanese undergraduates, *The Journal of Happiness Studies*, 2006, reported that not only did subjective happiness increase after counting one's acts of kindness but also that happier people became kinder and more grateful through the act of counting their acts of kindness.

Be kind: it's good for you

It is cheering to learn that, according to a 2010 study in *The Journal of Social Psychology*, those who performed acts of kindness or acts of novelty experienced an increase in life satisfaction. Participants were either assigned acts of kindness or acts of novelty, or nothing, to perform over a 10-day period. Pity those poor participants who weren't assigned these acts, for their satisfaction in life was not enhanced.

Go, kind people!

Be kind: science says so

Looking at it from a purely selfish point of view, scientists wondered whether being kind to strangers or close family members had more or less effect on the happiness of the kind-giver. 'Happily', a 2019 study in the *Journal of Social Psychology* reported that being kind to all people, regardless of whether they shared strong or weak social ties, had equally positive effects on happiness.

Neurologists report lively activity in the posterior superior temporal cortices of the brains of altruistic individuals.

The helper's high

While it's not exactly a scientific term, the helper's high has been identified as a physical rush of pleasure that occurs after indulging in a kind act. A 2006 research article into the neurology of donations found that the brain's mesolimbic reward system was stimulated by giving money as much as receiving it.

The triple effects of kindness

Being kind to someone in trouble helps more than just one person. Firstly, the kind act helps the afflicted; secondly, it helps the care-giver by provoking feelings of usefulness; thirdly, it inspires those around the kind person and encourages them to commit equally kind and useful acts.

Confucius on kindness

The Analects of Confucius are the sayings of the ancient Chinese sage Confucius, collected and recorded by his disciples. Very much like an ancient self-help book, *The Analects* comprises a series of maxims and sayings that helps people live a worthy life. Confucius considered kindness one of the essential attributes of a good person.

"To practise five things under all circumstances constitutes perfect virtue. These five are: gravity, generosity of soul, sincerity, earnestness and kindness."

CONFUCIUS
The Analects

Mozi on universal kindness

Over 2,500 years ago there lived a Chinese sage known as Mozi, or Mo Tzu, who preached universal love in a way that seems today strikingly modern. The concept of *jiān'ài* was developed, which focused the need on loving everybody, rather than just your immediate family, and committing acts of impartial caring. Mozi expressed exasperation that kindness to everyone was not endorsed by leaders – time barely seems to have changed!

"Now, as to universal love and mutual aid, they are beneficial and easy beyond a doubt. It seems to me that the only trouble is that there is no superior who encourages it."

MOZI

" I expect to pass through life but once. If therefore, there be any kindness I can show, or any good thing I can do to any fellow being, let me do it now, and not defer or neglect it, as I shall not pass this way again."

WILLIAM PENN

You may well have the kindest heart in the world, but if your heart doesn't move your mouth to speak kindness, your feet to walk where they are needed, nor your hands to shape kindness, your heart's kindness will remain your secret.

Become a RAKtivist

The Random Acts of Kindness Movement is recruiting more RAKtivists – people who believe that kindness can change the world. There are currently over 30,000 RAKtivists, representing nearly 90 countries. The kindness ambassadors are showered with inspiration and support to spread acts of kindness around the globe.

Let us be kind;
The way is long and lonely,
And human hearts are asking
for this blessing only –
That we be kind.
We cannot know the grief that
men may borrow
We cannot see the souls storm-
swept by sorrow,
But love can shine upon the way
to-day, to-morrow –
Let us be kind.

WALTER LOMAX CHILDRESS

Three easy acts of kindness

1. Buy a lottery ticket and give it to a stranger

2. Leave a pile of pennies by a fountain so people are able to make wishes

3. Offer to clean all the toys at the local playgroup

"You don't pay love back.
You pay it forward."

The Pay It Forward Movement is a new crusade of kindness based on an old idea of the eternal wave of good deeds. Catherine Ryan Hyde's *Pay It Forward* clarified the idea that if a good deed is done to you, rather than paying it back, you pay it forward to another in need. The result is ripples of kindness lapping around the world.

Five ways to pay it forward

1. If someone helps you when you've broken down, help someone when they've broken down

2. If someone loans you money, loan someone else money

3. If someone returns a lost item, seek the owner of a lost item

4. If someone lets you out at a junction, let another driver out later

5. If you receive a thoughtful compliment, pay someone else a compliment

Kind hearts are the gardens,
Kind thoughts are the roots,
Kind words are the blossoms,
Kind deeds are the fruits;
Love is the sweet sunshine
That warms into life,
For only in darkness
Grow hatred and strife.

ANONYMOUS

"A gentle word, a kind look, a good-natured smile can work wonders and accomplish miracles."

WILLIAM HAZLITT

Kindness is contagious –
be careful who you're kind
to – they might catch it.

Little acts of kindness
Trifling though they are,
How they serve to brighten
This dark world of care!
Little acts of kindness
Oh, how potent they,
To dispel the shadows
Of life's cloudy day!

ANONYMOUS

A little word in kindness spoken,
A motion or a tear,
Has often healed the heart
that's broken
And made a friend sincere.

DANIEL CLEMENT COLESWORTHY

Be kind to each other –
The night's coming on,
When friend and when brother
Perchance may be gone –
Then 'midst our dejection
How sweet to have earned
The blest recollection
Of kindness – returned! –
When day has departed,
And Memory keeps
Her watch, broken hearted,
Where all she loved sleeps! –

CHARLES SWAIN

Show kindness with flowers

When next sending a loved one, or yourself, a bouquet of flowers, choose blooms that symbolise kindness:

Anthurium: hospitality and kindness

Freesias: thoughtfulness, as well as sweetness and innocence

Gerbera daisies: cheerfulness

Gladioli: generosity

Elderflower: compassion

Yellow tulips: cheerful thoughts

"The greatest pleasure I know is to do a good action by stealth and have it found out by accident."

CHARLES LAMB

Five ways to be kind with money

1. Start a piggy bank for a charity

2. Collect your pennies and, after a year, take them to a bank and give the notes to someone of your choosing

3. Tip in coffee shops

4. Say 'keep the change'

5. Learn how to do the 'coin behind the ear trick' and let the young relatives or children of friends keep the coin – a big one!

Kind people...

Complain less

Compliment more

Disapprove less

Welcome more

Acquire less

Share more

The world is full of kind people...

If you can't find one, be one.

"Constant kindness can accomplish much. As the sun makes ice melt, kindness causes misunderstanding, mistrust and hostility to evaporate."

ALBERT SCHWEITZER

Kindness does not gloat

"Do not speak of your happiness to one less fortunate than yourself."

PLUTARCH

True kindness envelops the whole world. Be kind about your approach to the planet and walk softly. Foster good habits and honour the natural world by taking the time to appreciate its beauty.

Charity is institutionalised kindness

If you are a regular donor to charities, you might want to think about ways to pull your generosity closer, and thus take pleasure in your kindness yourself. Whether being kind to those in need, or the planet, try these acts in addition to your charitable commitments:

Cooking a meal for a
lonely neighbour

Volunteering with your
closest local charity

Giving blood

Buying and consuming less

Shopping and volunteering
in charity shops

Rehoming a rescue dog / cat

Giving to a food bank

"Kindness in words creates confidence. Kindness in thinking creates profoundness. Kindness in giving creates love."

LAO TZU

"We ought not to treat living creatures like shoes or household belongings, which when worn with use we throw away."

PLUTARCH

Let kindness lead you to a gentle relationship with animals. Carefully stroke cats and dogs when you meet them, find ways to invite pests out of your home without calling in vermin control, consider not eating animals.

"If you have men who will exclude any of God's creatures from the shelter of compassion and pity, you will have men who will deal likewise with their fellow men."

FRANCIS OF ASSISI

Ten ways to care for, and be in tune with, your environment

1. Learn how to use a glass and a postcard to capture helpless spiders, wasps or bees to release them outside

2. Join the Trillion Trees initiative to regrow, protect and plant one trillion trees by 2050

3. Remember the 3 Rs: Reduce, Reuse and Recycle

4. Take a bag and a pair of gloves with you to collect litter every time you take a walk

5. Drink tap water

6. Airdry clothes

7. Use LED light bulbs

8. Grow a garden and get involved with composting

9. Walk, bike, run

10. Take time to appreciate the majesty of our planet

"He that plants trees loves others beside himself."

THOMAS FULLER

Ubuntu – Southern African kindness to all humanity

Generally translated from the Nguni Bantu language to mean 'I am because we are', *ubuntu* is characterised as an African-specific form of humanism. Stressing that individuals find their humanity through others, ubuntu encourages the sharing of ourselves with others. From offering hospitality to recognising and embracing the humanity in fellow humans, ubuntu is a generous and joyful way to approach kindness to others.

Kaitiaki – Maori kindness to nature

Maoris, the indigenous people of New Zealand, have an ancient concept of *kaitiaki*, which refers to the concept of guarding the sky, sea and land. Maori origin legends have humans coming from both mother earth and the sky and, as a result, humans and nature are as one. According to this concept, nature has the same rights as humans and needs to be treated with equal kindness.

Japanese gifts of kindness

Japan has many gift-giving rituals that have evolved as ways of showing kindness and respect

Giri-choco – the giving of chocolate by women to all of their male co-workers on Valentine's Day

Omiyage – the bringing of souvenir presents following a trip

Ochugen – mid-year gifts to show gratitude to students, teachers or colleagues

Oseibo – end-of-year gifts to show indebtedness to someone for their support throughout the year

Free coffee in Italy

Caffè sospeso (suspended coffee) is an Italian tradition, over 100 years old, where someone buys a coffee but pays for two. That way, the next person to order a coffee is given one for free.

Tulong – to help, to assist – Filipino kindness

Practising *tulong* in the Philippines is practical kindness of the most useful type. Particularly effective after catastrophic events, tulong is the act of giving food, collecting clothing and providing practical help where you can.

The World Giving Index tracks which countries give most to charity and whose citizens volunteer the most.

In 2019 the most giving countries in the world were:

1. Indonesia
2. Australia
3. New Zealand
4. United States
5. Ireland
6. United Kingdom
7. Singapore
8. Kenya
9. Myanmar
10. Bahrain

A tale of old English kindness

In the 12th century Lady Mabella Tichborne lay dying in her home. She implored her husband to continue her tradition of donating farm produce to the poor. He said he would only donate produce from an area she was able to walk around with a lighted torch. The kindly Lady Mabella rose from her death bed and managed to crawl around a 23-acre field before the torch went out. She returned to bed and died, but the Tichborne Dole was born. The wheat from the field is still milled every year and given to parishioners of Tichborne.

"It is the characteristic of the magnanimous man to ask no favour but to be ready to do kindness to others."

ARISTOTLE

Don't listen to the naysayers – it is not true that 'a good deed never goes unpunished'.

Unvisited tombs of the kind

Dorothea Brooke is the heroine of George Eliot's Victorian masterpiece, *Middlemarch.* The novel charts Dorothea's struggle to live a useful life and to 'do good.' Eliot reminds readers of the numerous people who have lived quiet, decent and kind lives who are not now remembered, but whose influence invigorates all our lives.

"But the effect of [Dorothea's] being on those around her was incalculably diffusive: for the growing good of the world is partly dependent on unhistoric acts; and that things are not so ill with you and me as they might have been, is half owing to the number who lived faithfully a hidden life, and rest in unvisited tombs."

GEORGE ELIOT
Middlemarch

"Life is mostly froth and bubble,
Two things stand like stone,
Kindness in another's trouble,
Courage in your own."

ADAM LINDSAY GORDON

Twelve Days of Kindness

(To the tune of 'The Twelve Days of Christmas')

On the Twelfth Day of Kindness
I sent out to the world...

12 genuine compliments

11 beaming smiles

10 gifts of coffee

9 shifts of volunteering

8 handwritten notes

7 spontaneous hugs

6 calls home

5 random acts of kindness

4 offers of assistance

3 generous donations

2 teas with friends

And a hot bubble bath for me

*"Kindness is in our power
even when fondness is not."*

SAMUEL JOHNSON

Never mistake kindness for weakness.

While the ideals behind the 'random acts of kindness' movement are noble, to live a full and meaningful life, kindness should become our modus operandi. Rather than squeezing kindness in as another chore between everyday life activities, why not consider...

Always sending a complimentary note when you've enjoyed a great experience

Always opening doors for people

Always saying thank you and meaning it

Always making time to spend with people you love

Always smiling at those who serve you in shops and cafes

Be observant

Get in the habit of really observing your friends and family and noticing when they reveal their vulnerabilities or desires. Once you are tuned in to other people, you will be able to offer help without the recipient realising they have asked for it. Even the act of saying something along the lines of, 'I noticed you seemed a bit down the other evening, please let me know if there's anything you'd like to talk about,' can be a real balm.

*"Kind words do not cost much.
Yet they accomplish much."*

BLAISE PASCAL

20 ways of showing kindness within the home

1. Tidy up without being asked

2. Leave notes to your parents / flatmates saying how much you appreciate them

3. Leave notes to your children / flatmates saying how much you admire and love them

4. No matter how annoying they are being, decide for today to let it go

5. Bring breakfast to people in bed in the morning

6. Show genuine interest in your sibling's / parent's / children's / friend's hobby. Ask if they could teach you more about it

7. Go for a day without issuing instructions of any kind

8. Let one family member decide exactly what food is going to be eaten for a whole day

9. Decide not to grumble

10. Offer to do your sibling's / parent's / children's / flatmate's chores for the day

11. Say, 'Go and sit down, I'll clear up, it will be my pleasure.'

12. Say, 'Thank you,' without prompting

13. Say, 'I'm sorry I've made you cross, I'll try harder.'

14. Say, 'I love you.' (Even when you may not at that exact moment.)

15. Compliment your family members

16. Lock the door, draw the blinds, snuggle up and watch films all day. Yes, all day

17. Decide to say yes rather than no

18. Give your family members your full attention when they talk to you

19. Hug without limits

20. Forgive without qualification

Kindness is...

Intentional positive activity

Necessary to happiness

Decency

Needed more than ever

Energising

Solicitous

Sympathetic

Greet the day with intentional kindness

Start each day with a moment to yourself where you make the decision to be intentionally kind. You could either focus on your demeanour or a more specific act of kindness. If it helps to clarify the intention, jot down how you would like your kindness to manifest itself. If you haven't managed to be intentionally kind by nightfall, be kind to yourself and have another go tomorrow.

"Three things in human life are important. The first is to be kind. The second is to be kind. The third is to be kind."

HENRY JAMES

"For peace is not mere absence of war, but is a virtue that springs from a state of mind, a disposition for benevolence, confidence, justice."

BARUCH SPINOZA

When in doubt: be kind.

Be kind after the tragedy

Generally people are very kind to those who have experienced extreme unhappiness: a bereavement, a financial collapse or illness. However, after the early days of the unhappy episode, friends trickle away, flowers wilt and pies remain uneaten in the fridge. Sometimes real sadness can occur when the sufferer is truly alone and wondering what to do next. Be the person who continues to check in weeks and months after the initial tragedy.

"The kinder and more intelligent a person is, the more kindness he can find in other people. Kindness enriches our life; with kindness mysterious things become clear, difficult things become easy and dull things become cheerful."

LEO TOLSTOY

Be open to the risks of kindness

To be truly kind is to step
into somebody else's shoes
and walk with them through
hardship. To be kind is to
share the vulnerabilities and
pain of others. Be prepared
to experience sadness and
frustration as you help others.
Know, however, that in doing
so you are sharing their burden.
And hopefully in the future
they will do the same for you.

Kindness may be socially uncomfortable

The lonely. The grieving. The lost.
The poorly. All will be living closer
to you than may be comfortable.
All would benefit from small acts
of kindness from a neighbour.

"No one can live a happy life if he turns everything to his own purpose. Live for others if you want to live for yourself."

SENECA

"You can always give something even it if is only kindness."

ANNE FRANK

Kind hearts are the gardens,
Kind thoughts are the roots,
Kind words are the flowers,
Kind deeds are the fruits,
Take care of your garden
And keep out the weeds,
Fill it with sunshine,
Kind words, and Kind deeds.

HENRY WADSWORTH LONGFELLOW

"A tree is known by its fruit; a man by his deeds. A good deed is never lost; he who sows courtesy reaps friendship, and he who plants kindness gathers love."

SAINT BASIL

We may live in a society that celebrates the achievements of self-interest but that does not mean such individualistic behaviour is our natural state. Rather, men and women are social creatures who have built families, communities and civilisations by mutual co-operation. We should honour this natural sociability of man by making kindness our default setting.

"To be kind is the greatest measure of human happiness."

FRANCIS HUTCHESON

Five free ways to be kind

1. Message someone in your family and tell them that you love them

2. Pour water for others before pouring it for yourself

3. Let another driver take the convenient parking space

4. Greet your family and friends warmly when they return home

5. Comfort a close friend who is feeling down

Kindness makes you the most beautiful person in the world no matter what you look like.

It is kind to see individuals how they are rather than how we want them to be. It is kind to care for people just as we find them.

The golden rule

Kindness is central to all major world religions, humanism and human rights legislation. Its importance is often known as The Golden Rule:

Treat others as you would wish to be treated.

Dayā – the Hindu art of kindness

Dayā is the Sanskrit word for kindness or compassion and refers to the feelings of empathy towards the sufferings of others. Within Hinduism, particular emphasis is put on practising dayā towards not just humans but also animals, insects and plants.

This lovely Hindu story tells of kindness towards both animals and humans:

The holy man, Sant Śankardev was passing through a forest when he found a deer tangled in a hunter's net. Śankardev felt great compassion for the creature and released it from the net. However, he worried his action would cause the hunter to lose his livelihood. Before carrying on with his pilgrimage, the holy men left a gold coin in the net to compensate the hunter for the loss of the deer.

" The person who is always involved in good deeds experiences incessant divine happiness."

Hindu scriptures

Gemilut hasadim – Jewish acts of loving kindness

It is believed within Judaism that *gemilut hasadim* – acts of loving kindness – is a core social value. Gemilut hasadim requires personal involvement and the forging of meaningful connections with the person who is being helped, with nothing being expected in return. Acts of loving kindness are not to be viewed as one-off events but rather as acts to be incorporated into daily life.

"In three ways is kindness greater than charity. Charity is done with money; kindness can be either with one's person or one's money. Charity is for the poor; kindness can be done for either the poor or the rich. Charity is for the living; kindness can be done for the living or the dead."

Sukkah, Talmud

The Kabbalah Tree of Life shows
10 *sefirot* (emanations) whereby
the divine reveals itself. Number
four is the concept of *chesed*
which, though hard to translate
from Hebrew, means roughly
'a loving obligation to kindness'.
Within Judaism, chesed is one
of the primary virtues.

"The highest form of wisdom is kindness."

Talmud

"Your own soul is nourished when you are kind; it is destroyed when you are cruel."

PROVERBS
chapter 11, verse 17

"Kindness should become the natural way of life, not the exception."

THE BUDDHA

"When words are both true and kind they can change the world."

THE BUDDHA

"And if anyone wants to sue you and take your shirt, hand over your coat as well. If anyone forces you to go with them one mile, go with them two miles. Give to the one who asks you and do not turn away from the one who wants to borrow from you."

MATTHEW
chapter 5, verses 40–42

"But love your enemies, do good to them, and lend to them without expecting to get anything back."

LUKE
chapter 6, verse 35

Remember: kindness begets kindness.

"Love is patient, love is kind."

1 CORINTHIANS
chapter 13, verse 4

"And be ye kind to one another, tender-hearted, forgiving one another."

EPHESIANS
chapter 4, verse 32

"Therefore as God's chosen people holy and dearly loved, clothe yourselves with compassion, kindness, humility, gentleness and patience."

COLOSSIANS
chapter 3, verse 12

"Practise truth, contentment and kindness, this is the most excellent way of life."

Guru Granth Sahib

Langar – kindness on an industrial scale

The ability to turn the concept of kindness into a practical act of goodness is exemplified by Sikhs in their *gurdwaras* (temples) all over the world. Introduced by Guru Nanak in around 1500, the concept of *langar* – feeding whomever needed feeding – symbolised both charity and equality. Enter any Sikh temple today and you will be offered a delicious vegetarian meal.

The Sri Guru Singh Sabha in Southall, London is the largest gurdwara in the world outside of India. Its ethos is that: 'The *langar* (the free kitchen) hall provides food to all citizens of the community seven days a week and will be able to serve as many as 20,000 meals a week, in the continuous and unique Sikh tradition, where all are welcome (race, sex, colour and creed do not matter), the food is always free and always strictly vegetarian.'

The importance of kindness to mothers in Islam

The Prophet Mohammed was asked to whom he should show kindness and the Prophet replied, 'Your mother.' Asked who came next he replied, 'Your mother.' Asked who came next and he replied for the third time: 'Your mother.'

*"He who is deprived of kindness
is deprived of goodness."*

Islamic hadiths

The 5th-century Latin poet Prudentius wrote *Psychomachia,* an epic poem about the battle between good and evil. In it he identified the seven virtues that could fight against the seven deadly sins.

The seven virtues:

1. Chastity
2. Temperance
3. Charity
4. Diligence
5. Patience
6. Kindness
7. Humility

Cultivating kindness was thought by early medieval churchmen to be particularly good at fending off the deadly sin of envy.

It is easier to pass on love and kindness when you have received tons of both, but it is not a prerequisite to being kind. In fact, being kind is crucial if you are going to enter the eternal circle of kind-giver and kind-receiver. If anger, resentment and revenge have not produced the results you were hoping for, give kindness a chance.

Independence. Doing it for yourself. Autonomy. Resilience. Strength of character. Such are the expectations of adults today. In our modern age, it is only babies or the elderly who are allowed to rely on others to thrive. Yet, sorrow awaits anyone attempting to struggle through adult life without kindness and support from their fellow men and women.

"*No man is an island, entire of itself.
Every man is a piece of the continent.*"

JOHN DONNE

To assume that life can be led insulated from the emotions of others is to deny yourself the ability to experience the natural inclinations of your heart and your humanity.

The philosopher David Hume suggested that those who denied the existence of human kindness had 'forgotten the movements of his heart'.

The milk of human kindness

Kindness = milkiness: suitable only for children or the weak.

Lady Macbeth is to blame for associating kindness with weakness. Desperate for her husband, Macbeth, to seize the crown, she rages at him that he's 'too full o' th' milk of human kindness' to kill his rivals. As if being too kind was a frailty rather than a strength.

"Glamis thou art, and Cawdor, and shalt be
What thou art promis'd. Yet do I fear thy nature,
It is too full o' th' milk of human kindness
To catch the nearest way."

WILLIAM SHAKESPEARE
Macbeth

In the past, particularly the Victorian age, notions of kindness, especially female kindness, were lauded, admired and respected. Kind women were regarded as prestigious, and being kind was a virtue all girls should aim for. Today, kindness has a more understated and complicated role in what it means to be a woman. Girls are encouraged to be, 'strong', 'rebel women', 'difficult', 'daring' and 'different'. Kindness is seen as passive and submissive. This is unfair. Being kind is a strength, and no woman, in fact no person, should be embarrassed to be kind.

Being kind does not preclude bravery, strength or rebelliousness; it complements them. To be kind today is to be truly badass and brave.

Kindness is as important today as it was yesterday and will be tomorrow.

Be kind: it's expanding

Being kind to others takes us out of our comfort zone and into the lives of others. By actively being kind our own life is expanded, the range of people we have meaningful interactions with grows, and the emotions we experience become more kaleidoscopic in colour.

Kindness recognises human frailty

To be kind is to acknowledge the weakness and vulnerabilities of others. It is to recognise that life is hard, struggles are inevitable and that no one, no matter how privileged, has an easy time of it. To be kind is to accept the weakness of others, as well as yourself and do what you can to strengthen and support.

*"If you can't say anything nice...
don't say nothing at all."*

THUMPER
(the bunny with the noisy foot,
friend of Bambi)

But I'm not a kind person; how can I be kind?

There is a modern misconception that kindness is an inherent characteristic, in the same way that someone has blue eyes, another person is kind, or another selfish. This is not true. Kindness can be developed, it can be practised, it can become a habit, and once it's a habit it becomes a characteristic. By carrying out kind acts we become kind. Simples. After all...

"You are what you believe in. You become that which you believe you can become."

Bhagavad Gita

"Be kind, for everyone you meet is fighting a harder battle."

PLATO

One of the most poignant, even mournful evocations of kindness occurs in the song 'Auld Lang Syne' by Scottish poet Robert Burns. Often sung on New Year's Eve, the song speaks of sharing a cup of kindness with men and women to celebrate friendships and memories of times past. Whether coffee or a glass of wine, think about sharing a cup of kindness with friends today.

Whilst gazing upon the ruins of Tintern Abbey, Wordsworth contemplates man's demise and considers what remains after life expires.

He concludes: **kindness and love**.

I have owed to them
In hours of weariness, sensations sweet,
Felt in the blood, and felt along the
heart;
And passing even into my purer mind,
With tranquil restoration – feelings too
Of unremembered pleasure: such,
perhaps,
As may have had no trivial influence
On that best portion of a good man's
life,
His little, nameless, unremembered,
acts
Of kindness and of love.

WILLIAM WORDSWORTH
Lines Written a Few Miles above Tintern Abbey

Kindness can seem unattainable, as if only saintly figures such as Mother Theresa or Nelson Mandela or Princess Diana have the capacity for true kindness. But in fact, kindness is rather ordinary. It's making a cup of tea for your partner, it's picking up an empty chicken box and putting it in the bin, it's phoning your grandfather for a chat. There is nothing saintly or otherworldly about kindness, it is prosaic.

How to be kind online

- Call the person who is always updating their social media feed – they may be lonely

- Don't write anything online you wouldn't say out loud

- Spread love not hate – don't like negative comments

How to be kind online in the workplace

Avoid replying all

CC only with approval

Spend five minutes sending a complimentary email to one of your colleagues about their work and copy in their manager

Think twice before beginning any email – is there a kinder more efficient way for me to be relaying this information?

Kindness walks with bravery

Sometimes it is the case that so acute and immediate is suffering that kindness becomes not only necessary but a moral imperative. At times, to be kind can mean putting yourself in acute physical danger, with the threat of death a very real possibility. It is no wonder, when this level of extreme kindness is committed by individuals, that their names reverberate through history and they set an example to us all.

Kindness can be selfish and that's OK – Abraham Lincoln says so

That marvellous President Abraham Lincoln, freer of slaves and moral giant, was not so saintly that he would only commit kind acts for their own sake. In this little story published in 1898, Lincoln and his friend Colonel E. D. Baker were on a train discussing selfishness in doing good or evil. As the train passed over a bridge they saw an old razor-back sow on the bank of the slough (swamp) making a terrible noise because her pigs had got stuck and were in danger of drowning.

Lincoln asked for the train to be stopped, ran to the swamp and pulled the piglets out of the mud. When he returned his friend said:

"Now, Abe, where does selfishness come in in this little episode?"

Abraham Lincoln replied:
"Why, bless your soul, Ed, that was the very essence of selfishness. I would have had no peace of mind all day had I gone on and left that suffering old sow worrying over those pigs. I did it to get peace of mind don't you see?"

J. E. GALLAHER
Best Lincoln Stories – Tersely Told

Harriet Tubman – the rescuer of slaves

Born into slavery, Harriet Tubman escaped and helped rescue approximately 70 enslaved people.

Using the 'Underground Railroad', a loose system of safe houses and supporters, Harriet Tubman guided many slaves out of the state of Maryland to freedom in the northern American states. At constant risk, by officials and bloodhounds who were used to track fugitive slaves, Harriet Tubman, and all those she helped, evaded capture.

"If you hear the dogs, keep going. If you see the torches in the woods, keep going. If there's shouting after you, keep going. Don't ever stop. Keep going. If you want a taste of freedom, keep going."

HARRIET TUBMAN

Oskar Schindler – used kindness (and bribes) to defy a dictatorship

Made famous by Steven Spielberg's film, *Schindler's List*, Oskar Schindler's life was, in reality, no Hollywood film. His actions, in protecting 1,200 Jews in the teeth of a Nazi dictatorship, demanded kindness and bravery on an epic level. The German industrialist used his enamelware factory to protect those in danger. He bribed Nazi officials to allow Jewish workers to work for him rather than being sent to concentration camps.

He was a member of the Nazi party and used his connections to protect those the Nazi party wished to exterminate.

He and his wife Emilie were named 'Righteous Among the Nations' by the Israeli government in 1993.

Desmond Doss – pacifist who went to war

Combat medic Desmond Doss ran into desperately dangerous conditions to rescue 75 injured men during the Battle of Okinawa.

His unflinching kindness to those suffering earned him The Medal of Honour – the only one awarded to a conscientious objector. The film *Hacksaw Ridge* was made about his life and his example demonstrates why personal convictions are no barrier to extraordinary acts of kindness.

"You cannot do a kindness too soon because you never know how soon it will be too late."

RALPH WALDO EMERSON

Philanthropy – the kindness of the rich

Meaning 'love of humanity', philanthropy refers to generous kindness and charity on a large scale. Great wealth gives its owners enormous power to commit kind acts that can truly change the outcomes of individuals, families and, possibly, even the entire globe.

It is possible to be rich and kind.

Bill and Melinda Gates Foundation – kindness on a global scale

With the aim of giving away 95 percent of their wealth, The Bill and Melinda Gates foundation currently holds $50.1 billion – that's a lot of money to be kind with.

Its health, education and equality initiatives aim to improve the health and prospects of the whole planet. This is not the place for 'small acts of kindness'.

The foundation is working towards zero polio, zero malaria, zero tuberculosis, zero HIV, zero malnutrition, zero preventable deaths. And improving the education prospects for children the world over. And reducing inequality. And improving sanitation. And stopping sex trafficking. The Foundation is making headway in all regions.

Robert F. Smith – kindness to college students

Robert F. Smith, billionaire businessman, delighted the May 2019 graduation class at Morehouse College, Georgia, America when he joined them to receive an honorary degree. After his speech he announced that he would be paying off the student loans, not only of the students but also the parents of students who had taken out loans to fund their education. Over 400 students will benefit from his $34 million act of kind generosity. All he's asked the students to do is 'pay it forward'.

Banking billionaire funds kindness research

Billionaire Denny Sanford has given $100 million to research compassion. Inspired to discover how 'grace, humanity and kindness' can change the world, Sanford has funded the Sanford Institute for Empathy and Compassion. The institute aims to use cutting edge neurobiology 'to find the irrefutable scientific data that validates the immense power of compassion'.

Being kind costs nothing

1. Give your attention. All of it. For as long as is necessary

2. Listen. Properly. With both ears. Without interrupting

3. Hug for as long as it takes

4. Wipe away tears

5. Hold hands until the pain has gone

6. Turn up

7. Stand shoulder to shoulder

8. Bring laughter

9. Understand

10. Make time

"The value of a man resides in what he gives and not in what he is capable of receiving."

ALBERT EINSTEIN

To be kind is to be...

Generous with your compliments

Generous with your time

Generous with your laughter

Generous with your energy

Generous with your hospitality

Generous with your ability to forgive

To be kind is to be...

Gentle with your criticism

Gentle when in haste

Gentle with yourself

Don't forget to be kind to yourself

Be a friend to the person you are today – not the person you hope to become. That person, be they thinner, fatter, fitter, more successful, less stressed and so on, almost never arrives. So, don't wait. Be kind to who you are today.

Give yourself the gift of kindness and unwrap it every day.

Five ways to be kind to yourself

1. Learn to say no (kindly)

2. Learn to say yes to new experiences that will expand your reality

3. Learn to listen to your body and adjust the pace of life when required

4. Get a good night's sleep (7–9 hours)

5. Let yourself be loved

Don't just be good to others, be good to yourself too.

Kind people are...

Quick to help
Slow to judge

Quick to forgive
Slow to anger

Quick to smile
Slow to scowl

Quick to celebrate
Slow to condemn

Quick to praise
Slow to criticize

Quick to notice
Slow to moan

It's never too late to be kind

1. Write a letter of thanks to a teacher who inspired you

2. Ask the name of someone who you see every day but with whom you haven't yet truly connected

3. Apologise to your parents for your teenage behaviour

4. Make a particular effort to forge good relations with the colleague / family member who drives you mad

5. Sit down with a grandparent for a chat

Extreme kindness of the bodily variety

Donate your...

Body to science

hta.gov.uk

Blood

blood.co.uk

redcrossblood.org

Bone marrow

bbmr.co.uk

bethematch.org

Eggs

eggdonoramerica.com

hfea.gov.uk

Kidney

kidney.org.uk

kidney.org

Organs

organdonation.nhs.uk

organdonor.gov

Stem cells

anthonynolan.org

dkms.org

QUOTES ARE TAKEN FROM

Abraham Lincoln, 1809–1865, 16th President of the United States

Adam Lindsay Gordon, 1833–1870, Australian poet

Albert Einstein, 1879–1955, German American physicist and genius

Arthur Schopenhauer, 1788–1860, German philosopher

Albert Schweitzer, 1875–1965, theologian and winner of the Nobel Peace Prize

Anne Frank, 1929–1945, diarist who perished in Bergen-Belsen concentration camp

Aristotle, 384–322 BC, Greek philosopher

Baruch Spinoza, 1632–1677, Dutch philosopher

Saint Basil, 330–379, bishop of the early church

Henry Bergh, 1813–1888, founder of the American Society for the Prevention of Cruelty to Animals

Blaise Pascal, 1623–1662, French mathematician and theologian

Robert Burns, 1759–1796, Scottish poet and lyricist

Charles Kingsley, 1819–1875, English priest and author of *The Water Babies*

Charles Lamb, 1775–1834, English essayist and poet

Charles Swain, 1801–1874, English poet

Confucius, 551–479 BC, ancient Chinese sage

Daniel Clement Colesworthy, 1810–1893, American printer and poet

Desmond Doss, 1919–2006, conscientious objector who served as a combat medic in World War II

Saint Francis of Assisi, 1182–1226, patron saint of animals and the environment

Francis Hutcheson, 1694–1746, Ulster-Scottish philosopher

George Eliot, 1819–1880, English novelist and author of *Middlemarch*

Harriet Tubman, c. 1820–1913, American abolitionist

Henry James, 1843–1916, American-British author

Henry Wadsworth Longfellow, 1807–1882, American poet

John Donne, 1572–1631, English poet and cleric

Joseph Joubert, 1754–1824, French essayist

Lao Tzu, Ancient Chinese philosopher

Leo Tolstoy, 1828–1910, Russian author of *War and Peace*

Lily Hardy Hammond, 1859–1925 author of *In the Garden of Delight*

Mark Twain, 1835–1910, American novelist and author of *The Adventures of Tom Sawyer*

Martin Luther King Jr., 1929–1968, American minister and Civil Rights leader

Menachem Mendel Schneerson (aka Lubavitcher Rebbe), 1902–1994, American rabbi

Mozi, 470–391 BC, Ancient Chinese sage

Oskar Schindler, 1908–1974, German industrialist

Plato, 429–347 BC, Ancient Greek philosopher

Plutarch, AD 46–AD 120, Greek essayist

Ralph Waldo Emerson, 1803–1882, American essayist

Saint Teresa of Calcutta, Mother Teresa, 1910–1997, Albanian nun who devoted her life to caring for the poor

Samuel Johnson, 1709–1784, English lexicographer

Seneca, 4 BC–AD 65, Roman philosopher

Theodore Isaac Rubin, 1923–2019, American psychiatrist and author

Thumper, the rabbit with the noisy foot, friend of Bambi

Thomas Fuller, 1608–1661, English churchman

Walter Lomax Childress, 1867–1936, early 20th-century American minister

William Hazlitt, 1778–1830, English essayist

William Penn, 1644–1718, founder of Pennsylvani

William Shakespeare, 1564–1616, English playwright

William Wordsworth, 1770–1850, English romantic poet

BIBLIOGRAPHY AND FURTHER READING

A–Z of Almost Everything, by Trevor Montague, Little Brown, 2001

Best Lincoln Stories – Tersely Told, by J. E. Gallaher, 1898

Essays of William Hazlitt, selected and edited by Frank Carr, 1889

Jewish Traditions: A JPS Guide, by Ronald L. Eisenberg

On Kindness, by Adam Phillips & Barbara Taylor, Penguin, 2009

The Oxford Dictionary of Quotations, OUP, 1941

The King James Bible

Hadiths quoted from: Al-Mu'jam Al-Awsat 6067, Sahih Muslim 2592, Musnad Ahmad 8945, Abu dawud 5123, Abu dawud 5120

Scientific papers cited:

Buchanan, K. E. & Bardi A. (2010), 'Acts of Kindness and Acts of Novelty Affect Life Satisfaction', *The Journal of Social Psychology*, 150:3, 235–237.

Moll, J., Krueger, F., Zahn, R., Pardini, M., Oliveira-Souza, R & Grafman J. (2006), 'Human Fronto-mesolimbic Networks Guide Decisions about Charitable Donation', PNAS October 17, 2006 103 (42) 15623–15628. Edited by Raichle, M. E. Washington University School of Medicine.

Morishima, Y., Schunk, D., Bruhin, A., Ruff C., Fehr, E. (2012) 'Linking Brain Structure and Activation in Temporoparietal Junction to Explain the Neurobiology of Human Altruism', *Neuron*, 75:1, 73–79.

Otake, K., Shimai, S., Tanaka-Matsumi, J. *et al.* (2006), 'Happy People Become Happier through Kindness: A Counting Kindnesses Intervention', *Journal of Happiness Studies* 7: 361.

Rowland L & Curry, O. S. (2019), 'A Range of Kindness Activities Boost Happiness', *The Journal of Social Psychology*, 159:3, 340–343.

Tankersley, D., Stowe, C. & Huettel, S. (2007), 'Altruism is Associated with an Increased Neural Response to Agency', *Nature Neuroscience* 10, 150–151.

USEFUL WEBSITES

randomactsofkindness.org

medschool.ucsd.edu/vchs/compassion

payitforwardday.com

earthday.org

THANKS

Most of the research from this book came from interviewing numerous kind people and finding out what motivates them. Thank you for sharing your inspiring wisdom.

Publishing Director Sarah Lavelle
Assistant Editor Stacey Cleworth
Words Joanna Gray
Series Designer Emily Lapworth
Junior Designer Alicia House
Head of Production Stephen Lang
Production Controller Sinead Hering

Published in 2020 by Quadrille,
an imprint of Hardie Grant
Publishing

Quadrille
52–54 Southwark Street
London SE1 1UN
quadrille.com

The publisher has made every
effort to trace the copyright
holders. We apologise in advance
for any unintentional omissions
and would be pleased to insert the
appropriate acknowledgement in
any subsequent edition.

Cataloguing in Publication Data:
a catalogue record for this book is
available from the British Library.

ISBN 978 1 78713 605 2

Printed in China